I0817987

eyewonder

Volcanoes

Senior Editor Kritika Gupta
Project Art Editor Heena Sharma
US Senior Editor Shannon Beatty
Picture Researcher Ridhima Sikka
Managing Editor Kingshuk Ghoshal
Managing Art Editors Anna Hall, Govind Mittal
Pre-production Team Vijay Kandwal
Production Editor Anita Yadav
Production Controller Magdalena Bojko
Project Jackets Art Editor Vidushi Chaudhry
India Creative Head Malavika Talukder
Associate Publisher Gemma Farr
Art Director Mabel Chan

Consultant Dr. Gill Jolly

This American Edition, 2026
First American Edition, 2003
Published in the United States by DK Publishing,
a division of Penguin Random House LLC
1745 Broadway, 20th Floor, New York, NY 10019

26 27 28 29 30 10 9 8 7 6 5 4 3 2 1
001–358046–Jun/2026

Published in Great Britain by Dorling Kindersley Limited

ISBN 979-8-2173-0574-2

DK books are available at special discounts when purchased in bulk for sales promotions, premiums, fund-raising, or educational use. For details, contact: DK Publishing Special Markets, 1745 Broadway, 20th Floor, New York, NY 10019
SpecialSales@dk.com

Printed and bound in China

www.dk.com

This book was made with Forest Stewardship Council™ certified paper—one small step in DK's commitment to a sustainable future.
Learn more at www.dk.com/uk/information/sustainability

Contents

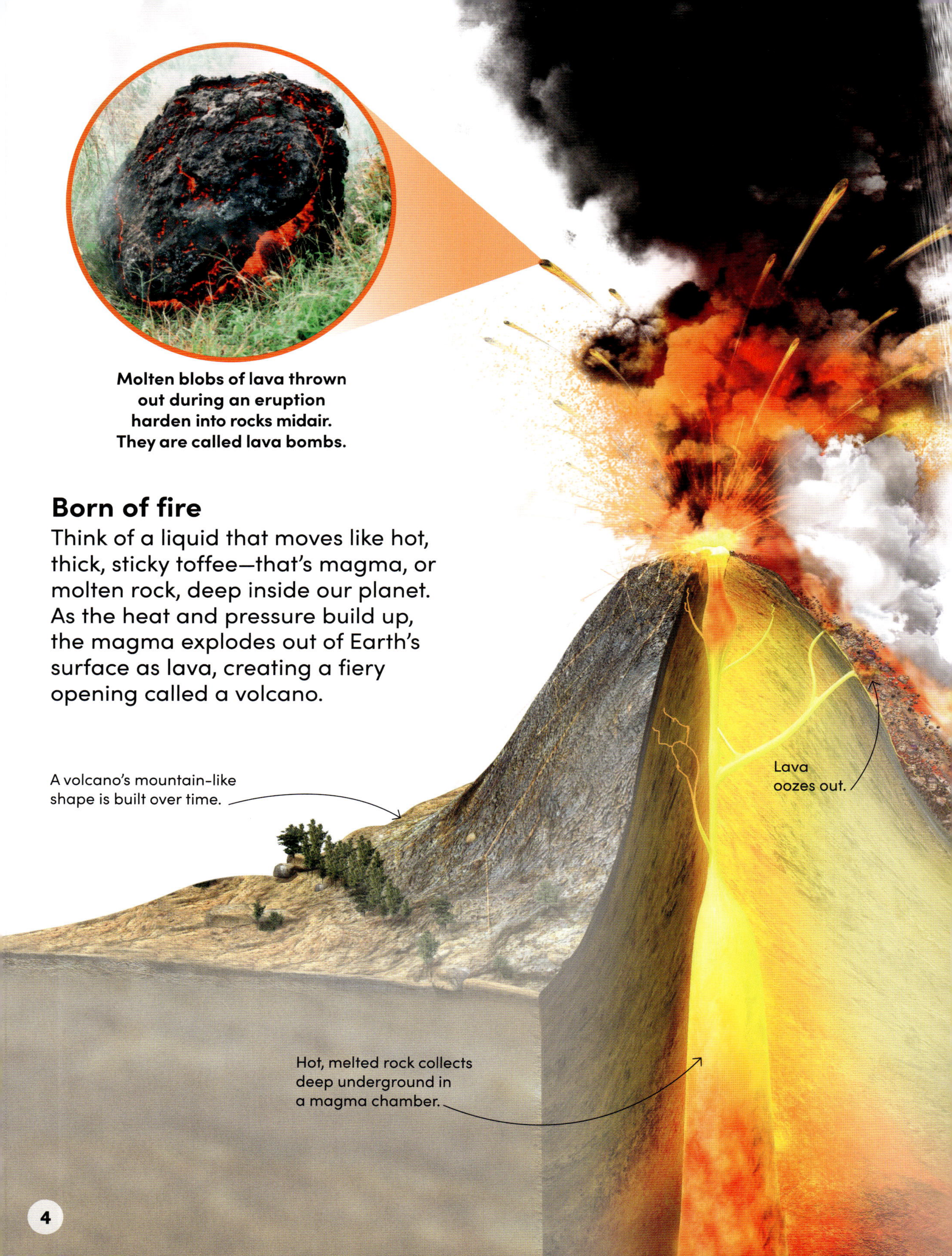

Molten blobs of lava thrown out during an eruption harden into rocks midair. They are called lava bombs.

Born of fire

Think of a liquid that moves like hot, thick, sticky toffee—that's magma, or molten rock, deep inside our planet. As the heat and pressure build up, the magma explodes out of Earth's surface as lava, creating a fiery opening called a volcano.

Spitting fire

Nothing on Earth roars quite like a volcano bursting into life! Huge eruptions spit out ash, stinky gases, and fiery rivers of lava. As the lava cools, it hardens into rock, forming new land.

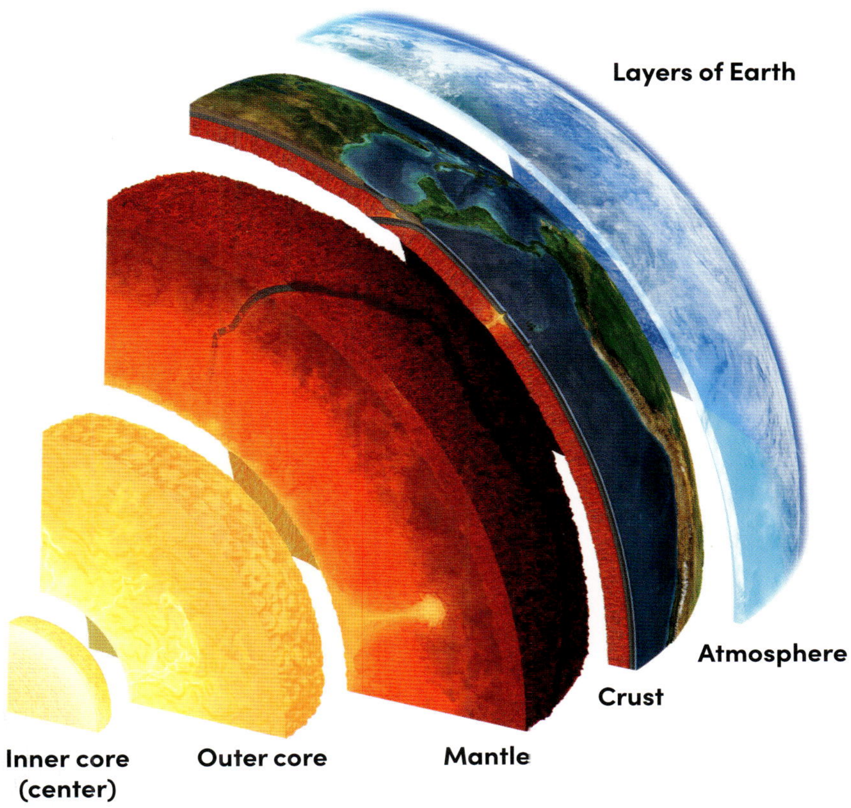

Layer by layer

Our planet is made up of many layers, just like an onion. These layers are made of rock and metal. The heat from Earth's core melts the rock in the mantle to make magma.

MAGMA MATTERS

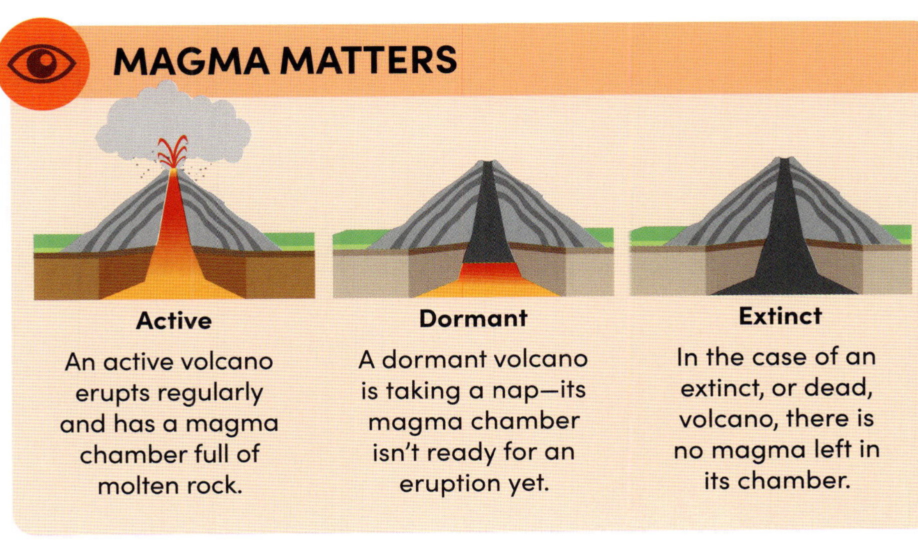

Active

An active volcano erupts regularly and has a magma chamber full of molten rock.

Dormant

A dormant volcano is taking a nap—its magma chamber isn't ready for an eruption yet.

Extinct

In the case of an extinct, or dead, volcano, there is no magma left in its chamber.

Rocky jigsaw

Earth's crust is broken into giant pieces that fit together like a jigsaw puzzle. These pieces are called tectonic plates. They move slowly, bumping against each other or pulling apart. Volcanoes happen at the places where two plates meet.

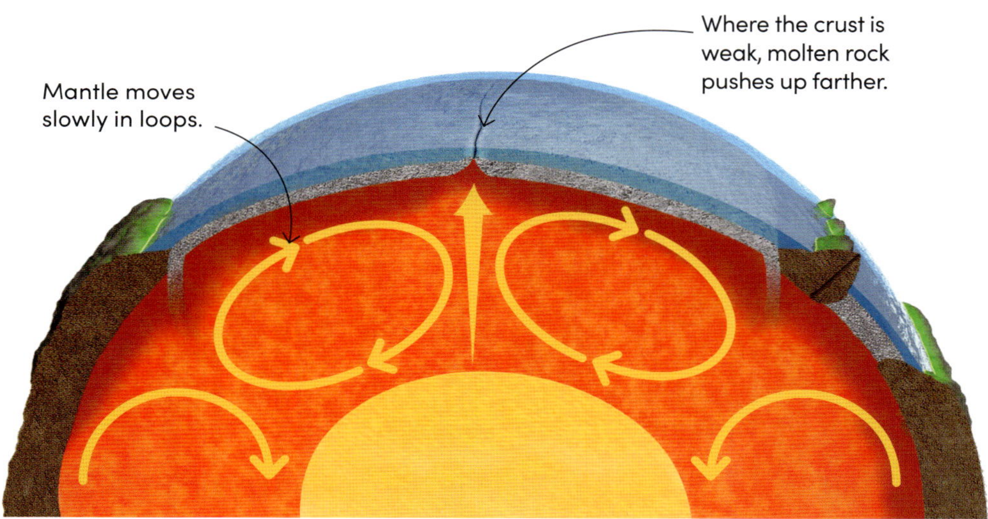

Rise and fall

Heat from Earth's core makes the molten rock of the mantle rise, but as it nears the surface it cools and falls again. This swirling motion shifts the plates, causing quakes and fiery eruptions.

Satellite view of the Rift Valley in Africa

Cracks in land in the rift region

Drifting apart

The Rift Valley is a region where the African tectonic plate is splitting in two slowly. This vast rift runs nearly 4,000 miles (6,400 km).

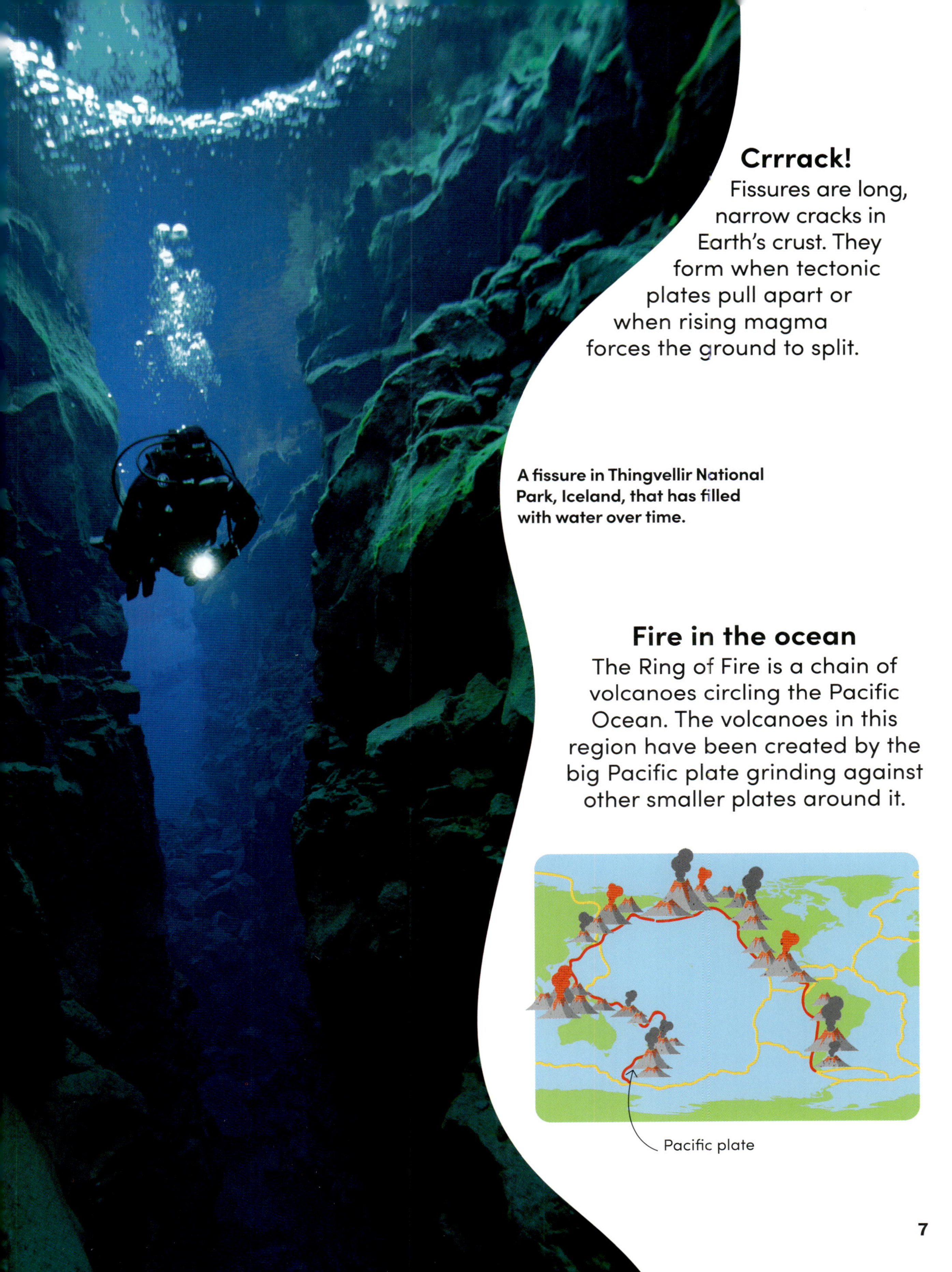

Crrrack!

Fissures are long, narrow cracks in Earth's crust. They form when tectonic plates pull apart or when rising magma forces the ground to split.

A fissure in Thingvellir National Park, Iceland, that has filled with water over time.

Fire in the ocean

The Ring of Fire is a chain of volcanoes circling the Pacific Ocean. The volcanoes in this region have been created by the big Pacific plate grinding against other smaller plates around it.

Boiling over

When water meets magma underground, it becomes boiling steam. This may erupt out of the ground as a scorching fountain, called a geyser. Elsewhere, it may mix with soil or rotten rock to form bubbling mud or acid pools.

Boiling mud

Gases released by hot magma may mix with underground water, soft clay, and minerals. This forms a bubbling pool of hot mud that hisses and steams.

Different colors in acid pools come from different minerals.

One of the world's most acidic pools is in the Danakil Depression, Ethiopia.

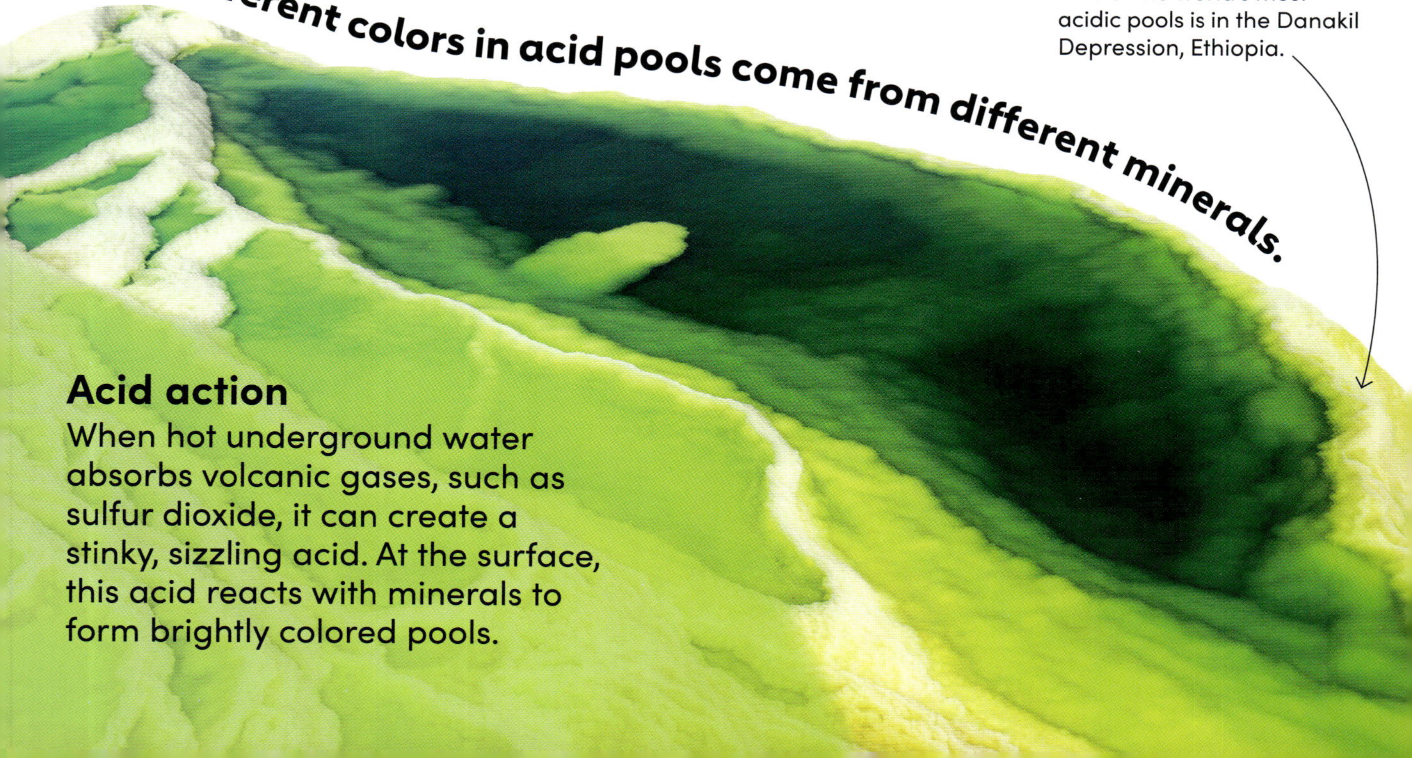

Acid action

When hot underground water absorbs volcanic gases, such as sulfur dioxide, it can create a stinky, sizzling acid. At the surface, this acid reacts with minerals to form brightly colored pools.

Steamy spring

Hot springs, such as the Grand Prismatic Spring in the United States, are natural pools of water warmed by heat from deep inside the planet.

Tiny heat-loving life forms make a rainbow of colors.

Steam in a geyser can be much hotter than water boiling in a kettle.

Whooosh!

A geyser is a special kind of hot spring that spurts jets of boiling water and steam into the air. The Fly Geyser in Nevada has tall mounds that formed as minerals in the water built up around the mouth of the geyser.

Meet the volcanoes

When you think of a volcano, you might picture a tall, pointy mountain. But volcanoes are not all the same—they can have different shapes and sizes.

The famous Japanese stratovolcano called Mount Fuji is 12,389 ft (3,776 m) tall.

Stratovolcano

The largest volcanoes are towering structures built by layers of lava and ash. Their eruptions can be powerful, spewing out fast-moving ash clouds and slow-moving rivers of lava.

Caldera

After an eruption, the magma chamber beneath the volcano may be empty. If the volcano collapses in on itself, it makes a hollow, called a caldera.

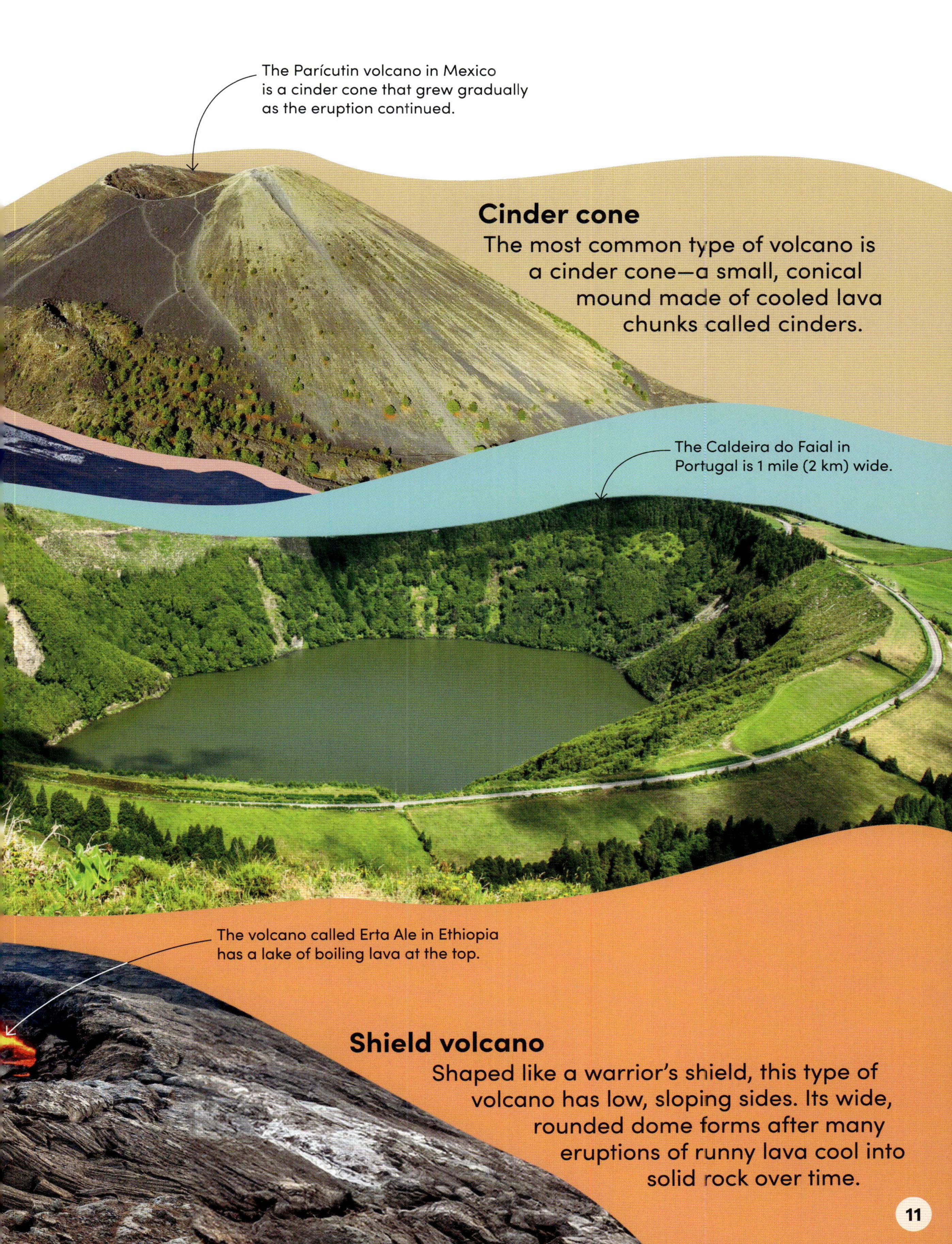

Cinder cone

The most common type of volcano is a cinder cone—a small, conical mound made of cooled lava chunks called cinders.

Shield volcano

Shaped like a warrior's shield, this type of volcano has low, sloping sides. Its wide, rounded dome forms after many eruptions of runny lava cool into solid rock over time.

Dead or alive?

Volcanoes are unpredictable—sleeping one moment and furious the next. Some can lay dormant or inactive for hundreds or thousands of years before roaring back to life. Others erupt frequently, unleashing lava, ash, and gases.

Fast facts

Japan's Mount Fuji is actually made up of three volcanoes.

Russia's Krasheninnikov volcanoes are named after the 17th-century explorer Stepan Krasheninnikov.

In 2025, Ethiopia's Hayli Gubbi volcano erupted for the first time in over 8,000 years.

A long sleep

A pair of volcanoes known as Krasheninnikov, in eastern Russia, lay dormant for more than 500 years before they woke up with a start in 2025. A huge earthquake nearby acted like their alarm clock!

Dormant giant

Mount Fuji has been dormant since 1770, but could come to life again at any time. This would be devastating for the millions of people in the city of Tokyo, just 60 miles (97 km) away.

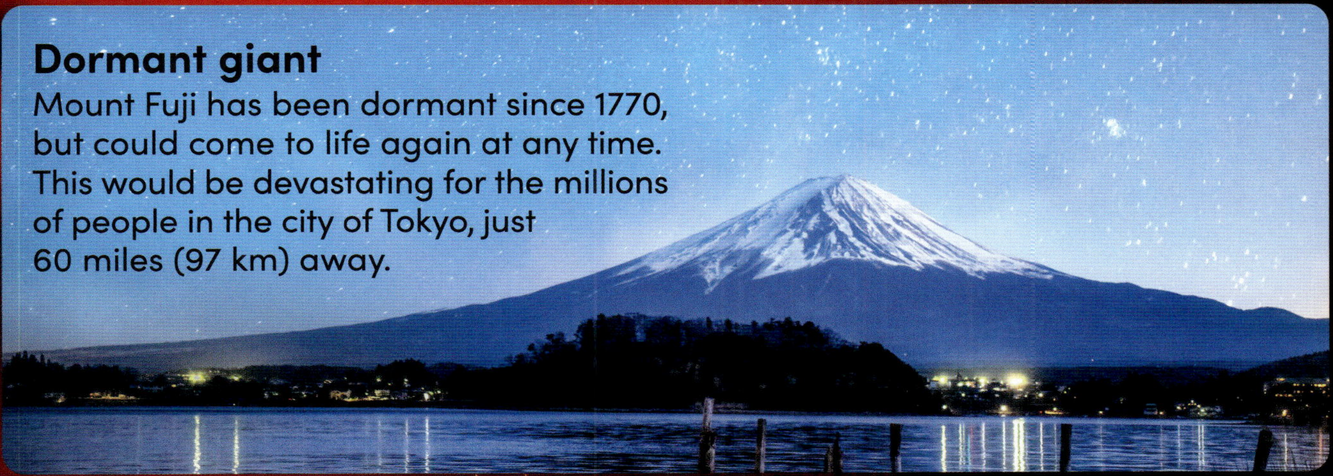

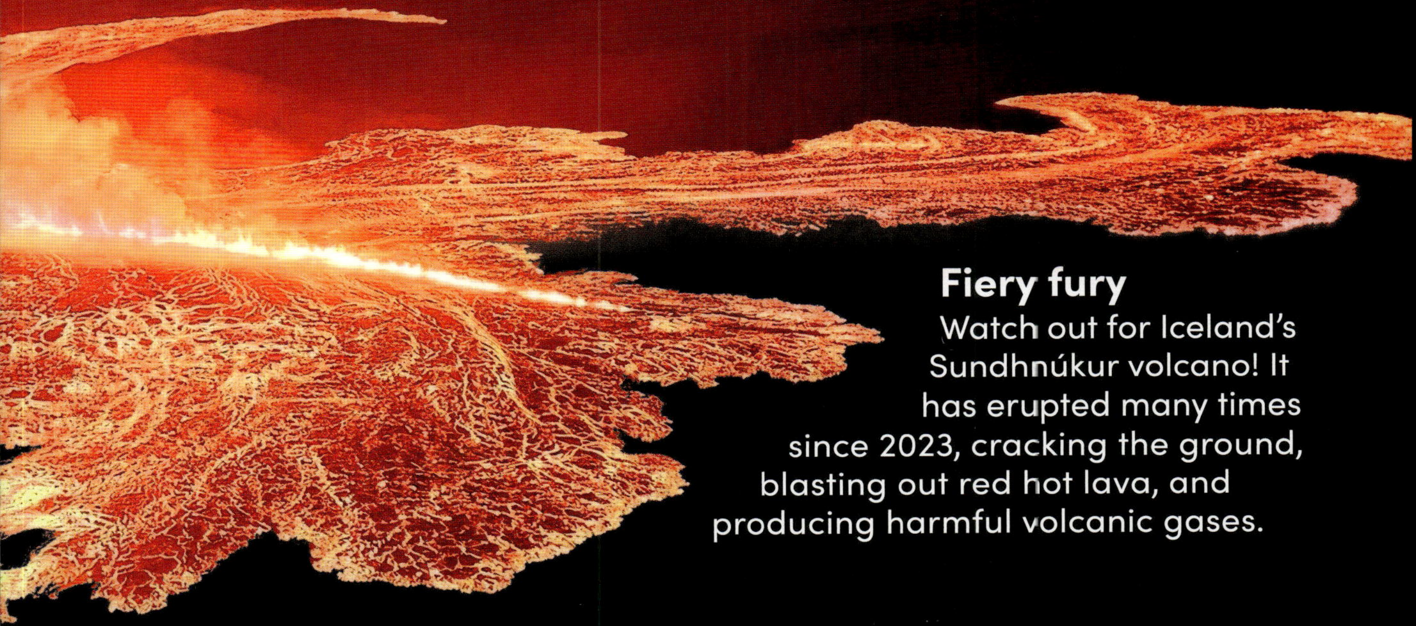

Fiery fury

Watch out for Iceland's Sundhnúkur volcano! It has erupted many times since 2023, cracking the ground, blasting out red hot lava, and producing harmful volcanic gases.

Signs of life

Mount Spurr in the USA hasn't erupted since 1992, but started showing signs of waking up in 2024—small tremors, escaping gas, and shifting ground. One day, it might erupt again.

In 2024, a new steaming lake formed near Mount Spurr's crater.

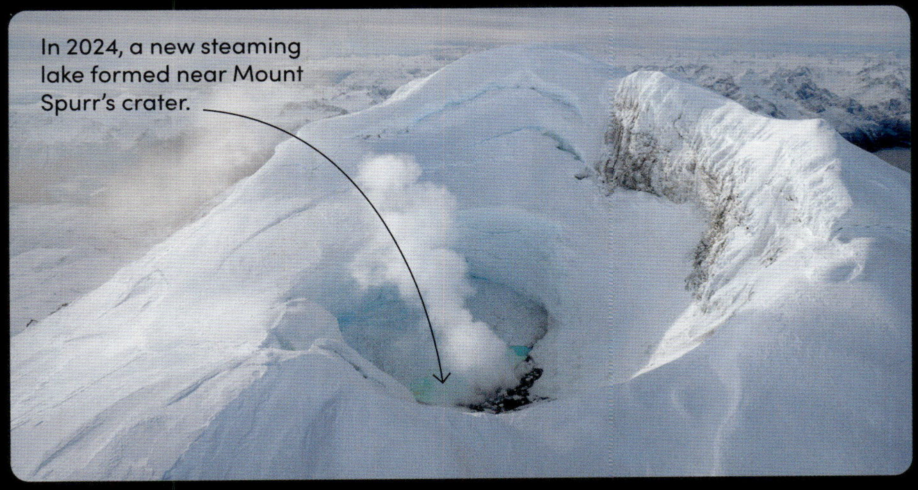

Red-hot rivers

When a volcano erupts, hot liquid rock called magma explodes outward or flows on the ground. Once it escapes the volcano, the flaming hot rock is called lava. It can burn everything in its path.

Fast facts

The temperature of some kinds of lava is seven to twelve times that of boiling water.

Lava can form many different shapes, such as cones, tubes, and even strands as fine as hair!

The words "aa" (ah-ah) and "pahoehoe" (pa-HO-ee-HO-ee) come from the Hawaiian language.

Exploding out

Sometimes, the magma is under a lot of pressure underground. This makes it spurt or explode out of the volcano, as lava.

As lava cools, it forms a hard, rocky "skin".

Flowing fire

Hot lava glows brightly as it oozes out of volcanoes. It thickens as it cools, but because this happens very slowly, it can cover hundreds of miles before it stops running.

Obsidian has a glass-like shine.

Pumice is light and full of tiny holes.

Basalt is a hard, dark-colored rock.

Igneous rocks

When hot lava cools down, it turns into a type of rock called igneous rock. Some of it forms deep underground, while some of it cools on Earth's surface. Each type of igneous rock has a unique shape and color.

Lava flow can cover almost 240 soccer fields in an hour!

Aa lava is rubbly and jagged.

Pahoehoe is swirly and smooth.

Block lava is large and chunky.

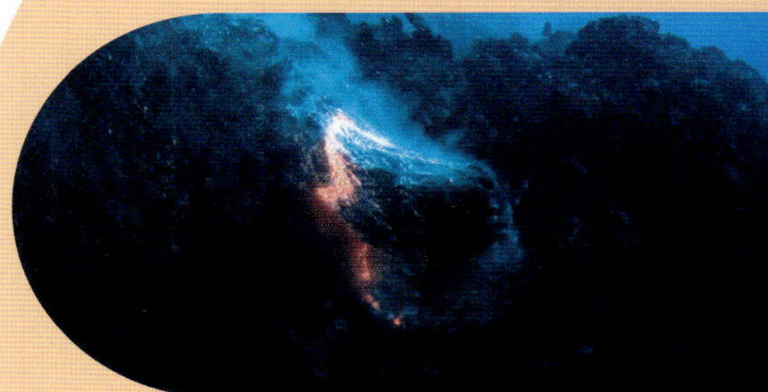

Pillow lava is rounded.

Lots of lava

Lava isn't all the same—it can be thick and sticky, or thin and runny. Much of it forms on the ground, but pillow lava forms under water.

Volcano watch

Scientists have ways to track volcanic activity and forecast where and when an eruption may occur. There is no way to stop it though—as magma rises, the pressure increases until... BOOM!

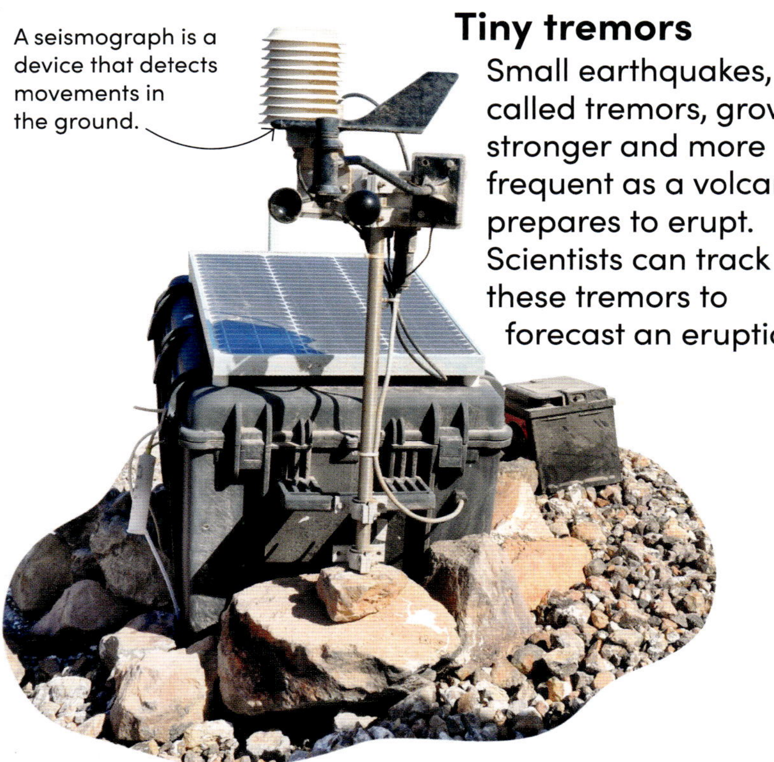

A seismograph is a device that detects movements in the ground.

Tiny tremors

Small earthquakes, called tremors, grow stronger and more frequent as a volcano prepares to erupt. Scientists can track these tremors to forecast an eruption.

Fast facts

Scientists study the temperature and water in crater lakes on active volcanoes to check for signs of volcanic activity.

Sometimes volcanoes can swell up or sink in right before an eruption.

Changes in a volcano are often monitored to provide early warning signs.

Steam vents (openings) near an active volcano let out clouds of volcanic gases.

Smelly signal

Sniff, sniff... does it smell like rotten eggs? That is hydrogen sulfide. It is released into the air with other gases when magma is nearing the surface.

Kaboom!

Shaking ground, stinky gases, and changes in the shape of a volcano all point to a possible eruption. When the pressure of the rising magma is too much for the ground to hold, ash, gas, and lava explode out in a volcanic eruption.

Every year, about 60 volcanoes erupt across the globe.

TYPES OF ERUPTION

How a volcano erupts depends on the amount of gas trapped inside the magma and how sticky the lava is. Based on this, a volcanic eruption may be effusive or explosive.

Runny lava flowing out gently

Effusive

Less gas means a gentler eruption—this is called an effusive eruption.

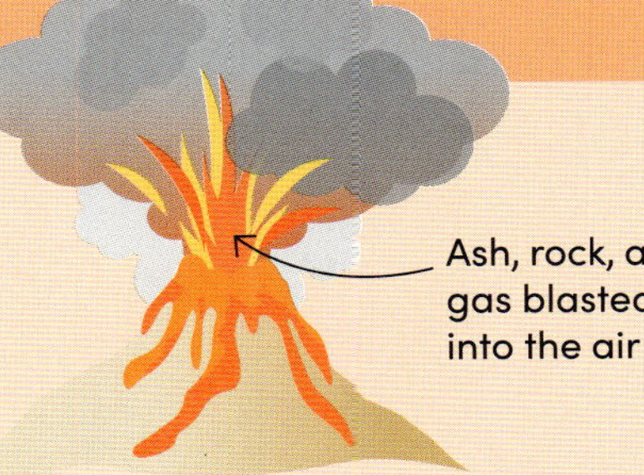

Ash, rock, and gas blasted high into the air

Explosive

When lots of gas is trapped in magma, the eruption is bigger. This is called an explosive eruption.

A failed rescue

When Mount Vesuvius erupted, Pliny the Elder, head of the Roman navy, saw the explosion from a nearby coastal town. He led a rescue attempt, but died in Pompeii after breathing in poisonous gases.

Preserved in ash

When Pompeii was dug up in the 1700s, archaeologists found food that had been preserved for almost 2,000 years!

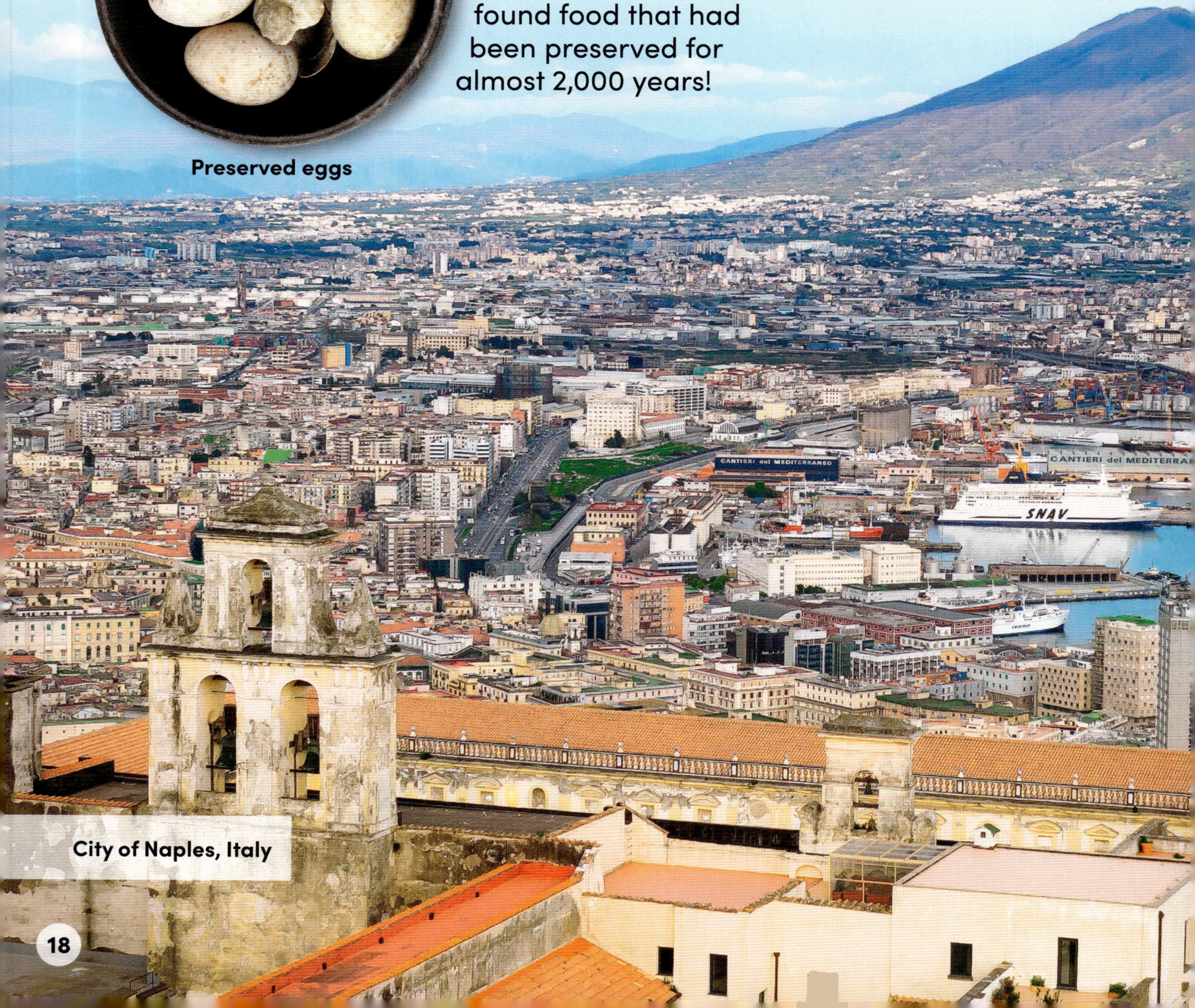

Preserved eggs

City of Naples, Italy

Pompeii

The ancient town of Pompeii in Italy was frozen in time by an eruption of Mount Vesuvius one morning in late 79 CE. It didn't take long for the entire town and its people to be buried under ash, dust, and lava.

Victims of Vesuvius

The eruption of Vesuvius killed many people, leaving behind body-shaped holes in the ash-covered ground. These were filled with plaster by archaeologists to create lifelike casts of the dead.

Ruins of Pompeii

Sleeping beast

Today, Mount Vesuvius may look quiet, but it has erupted many times since 79 CE. An eruption in 1944 lasted 10 days. Only a few people were hurt.

Light show

During some eruptions, the sky turns into a light show. Tiny pieces of lava in ash clouds rub together, creating an electrical charge. These charges then flash through the clouds as bolts of lightning.

Megaflashes of lightning from volcanic eruption can quickly cover over 19 miles (30 km).

The ash from the 1997 eruption of the Soufrière Hills volcano in the eastern Caribbean buried homes and cars.

Ash attack

Fine volcanic ash from eruptions can travel far on the wind, and cover entire regions in a blanket—like snow, but gray and nasty. This may force people living there to flee.

A volcano called Cordón Caulle erupts in Chile.

Volcanic weather

A violent volcano doesn't just shake the ground—it changes the sky, too. Monstrous clouds of ash and dust are hurled out during a volcanic eruption. This pollutes the air and blocks sunlight, making the weather cooler.

MUD FLOWS

Volcanic ash and rock can mix with water after heavy rainfall and sweep down a volcano's sides as a mud flow. It can quickly become a muddy river, full of debris.

Mega wave

When a volcano erupts under the sea, large parts of the ocean floor are lifted up, moving a lot of water and creating a tsunami. A massive undersea earthquake might do the same thing.

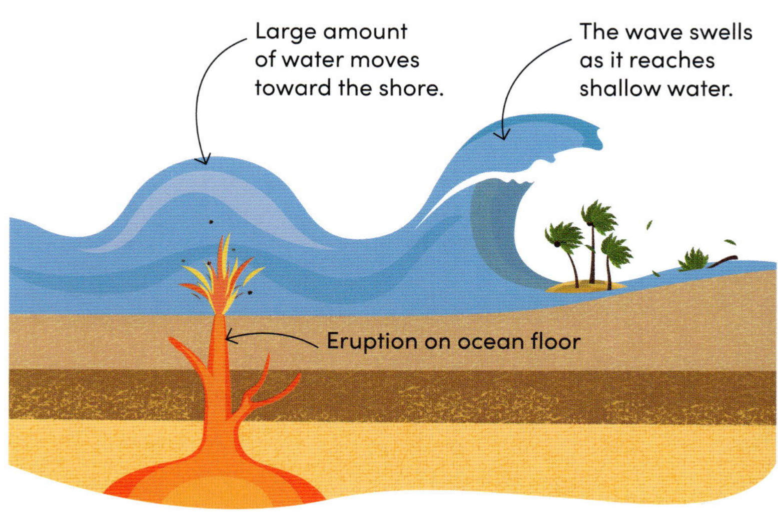

Fire in the ocean

In 2018, Indonesia's Anak Krakatoa volcano erupted and partly collapsed into the sea. The eruption and landslide triggered a deadly tsunami.

The 2018 eruption caused the volcano to lose over two-thirds of its size.

Hitting land

A tsunami can travel at speeds of up to 500 mph (805 kph) at sea, with enough power to sweep away entire coastal towns or villages. In 2011, a 98-ft- (30-m-) tall tsunami hit the Pacific coast of Japan, washing away everything up to 3 miles (5 km) inland. It was triggered by an undersea earthquake.

Tsunami

A tsunami is an enormous wave that can destroy everything in its path when it hits land. Often set off by an underwater volcanic eruption, it starts as wide, gentle ripples, which grow into a mighty wall of water.

Warning!
Tsunamis are hard to predict, but scientists use special floating tools, called buoys, to watch the waves. This is an early warning system!

An island is born

When a volcano erupts beneath the waves, lava piles up as it hardens on the ocean floor. Eruption after eruption makes this mound grow taller, until one day, its peak emerges from the water as an island.

Surtsey

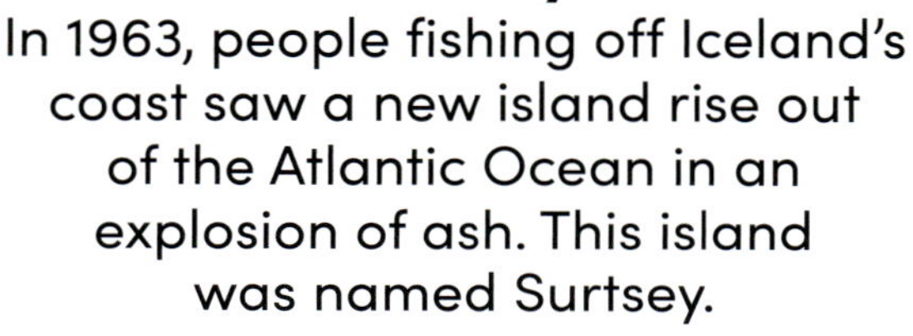

In 1963, people fishing off Iceland's coast saw a new island rise out of the Atlantic Ocean in an explosion of ash. This island was named Surtsey.

Life under water

As an underwater volcano grows, its rocky slopes become home to all kinds of marine life. Scientists studying the volcano have a chance to see fiery eruptions as well as amazing life-forms.

Home, sweet home

The Galápagos Islands, off the coast of South America, are volcanic islands that broke the surface of the water about 4 million years ago. Many types of animals, found nowhere else in the world, live on these islands.

Flightless cormorant

Marine iguana

Hidden beneath

Even a small island may look large, but it is just the tip of a hidden giant. Beneath the waves, the island is larger still!

Fiery curtain

In 1973, the Eldfell (ELD-fell) volcano rocked the Icelandic island of Heimaey. Lava fountains spurted from cracks in the volcano during the eruption, forming a curtain of fire.

Lava land

Iceland is one of the most volcanic places on the planet—it has more than 120 volcanoes! Deep beneath its snowy surface, molten magma builds up pressure, waiting to burst out.

Buried in black

Most of Heimaey's 5,300 residents escaped to the mainland as the volcano erupted. The island's buildings were buried in black ash.

Dark skies

In March 2010, a volcano named Eyjafjallajökull (AY-uh-fyat-luh-YOE-kuutl [-uh]) began erupting. The ash thrown out spread over the skies of northern Europe, grounding planes in many countries.

Volcanic ash darkened the skies.

STEAM POWER

Iceland's volcanoes don't just rumble—they help, too. The underground heat warms pools, like the one below in Grindavík (GRIN-da-veek), where everyone can bathe and relax. Nearby, a power plant turns the steam and hot water into clean electricity. This lights homes, schools, and other buildings.

Molten mayhem

Although it had been quiet for nearly 6,000 years, the Fagradalsfjall (FAH-grah-dalss-fyatl) volcano woke up in 2021. It erupted again in 2022 and 2023, and may erupt in the future.

Molten lava can reach a sizzling 2,200°F (1,200°C)!

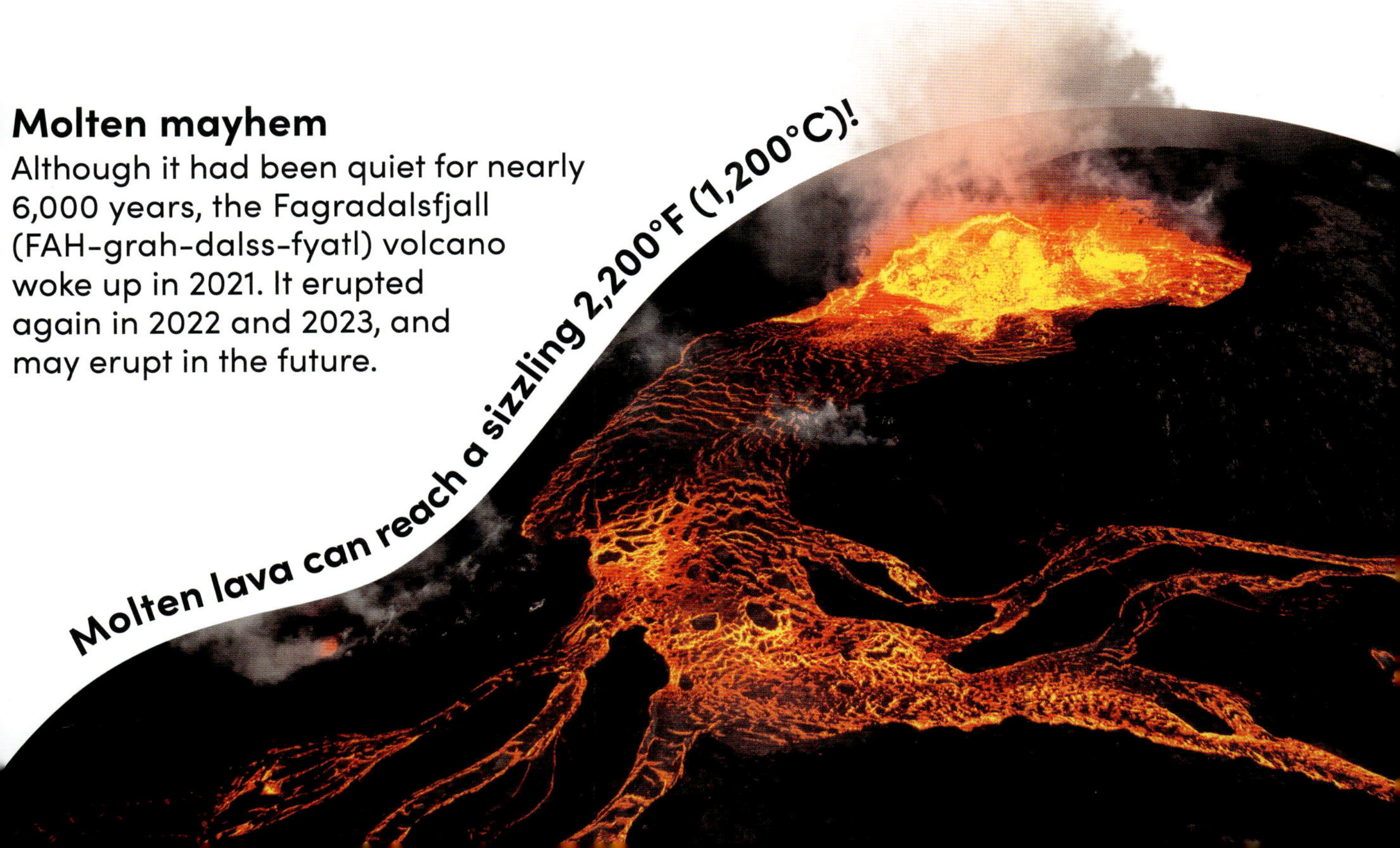

Fire and ice

Mount Erebus in Antarctica is the world's southernmost active volcano. It has a permanent lava lake—one of only a few long-lasting lava lakes in the world!

Mount Ijen's crater is about 1,100 ft (335 m) across.

Blue fire

Mount Ijen in East Java, Indonesia, is an active volcano with an acidic lake and a sulfur mine. It is known to give off sulfur gases, which mix with oxygen in the air, to make striking blue flames.

Ring of Fire

Earth's largest ocean is the Pacific Ocean. Surrounding it is a region of active volcanoes that dot many islands. Parts of our planet's crust—called tectonic plates—meet along this horseshoe-like "ring." It crackles with underground magma.

Volcanic islands

Nearly 57 volcanoes line the Aleutian Islands, which is a chain of more than 300 small islands off the coast of Alaska. Most of the islands were formed after volcanic eruptions.

The blue flames can be seen at night—they're too dim to be visible during the day.

Seeking sulfur

Mount Ijen's eruptions bring valuable elements, such as sulfur, close to the surface, where they are easy to mine.

Steaming spas

During the snowy winters in Japan, monkeys called Japanese macaques jump into hot springs to keep warm! The water helps to soothe and relax them.

Hot springs are often heated by magma underground.

Heat seekers

Living close to an active volcano might sound unwise, or even a little scary. Yet some animals survive—and even thrive—near volcanoes or volcanic heat.

Deep-sea thriver

Deep in the dark ocean, giant tube worms cluster around hydrothermal vents. These are cracks in the ocean floor that release hot, chemical-rich water.

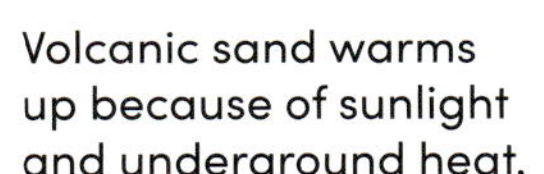

Volcanic sand warms up because of sunlight and underground heat.

Snuggly in sand

Many birds have to sit on their eggs to keep them warm, but not the clever maleo bird. It buries its eggs in volcanic sand, which keeps them warm.

Lava lizards

The Galápagos Islands in the Pacific Ocean are home to the lava lizard. Its dark skin looks like the volcanic rocks of its surroundings, helping it blend in.

Female lava lizards have reddish markings on the head and throat.

Yellowstone National Park

Geysers are fountains of hot water and steam.

Mantle plume rises

Satellite view of New Zealand's Lake Taupō, which formed over a caldera from a supervolcano eruption 26,000 years ago.

Rising magma

Supervolcanoes can be found in places where a large blob of hot magma rises and collects steadily over a long time. Gigantic chambers form beneath the surface, such as the one in Yellowstone in the United States.

Supervolcano

Supersized, superpowerful volcanoes are called supervolcanoes. When they erupt, they eject thousands of times more material than typical volcanoes. The last supervolcano eruption happened nearly 26,000 years ago.

This layer of volcanic ash was deposited about 1.3 million years ago.

Recorded in rock

So much ash is released by a supervolcano that it can cover huge areas of land. We know this because thick layers have been found preserved in rock.

That sinking feeling

When a supervolcano erupts, so much material comes out that the land collapses into the giant empty magma chamber. This creates a huge hole, called a caldera.

Lake Taupō

The Deccan Traps are made up mainly of basalt, a dark-colored volcanic rock.

Magma mountains

Supervolcanic eruptions can change huge areas of land, such as the mountainous Deccan Traps in western India. These were made by eruptions around 66 million years ago.

Life around a volcano

Volcanoes are explosive and unpredictable, which makes them dangerous to be around. Yet in many places, people live side-by-side with volcanoes, flourishing in their shadow while making sure to stay safe.

Helmets on

The Sakurajima volcano in Japan erupts often, hurling ash and lava rocks into the air. Local children wear hard hats outside their home for their safety.

Yadnya Kasada is an annual Tenggerese festival held near Mount Bromo, Indonesia.

VOLCANO GODDESS

In Indigenous Hawaiians beliefs, the spirit of the volcano goddess Pele dwells in the burbling, boiling crater of the volcano called Kīlauea. When she gets angry, the volcano erupts with her fiery rage.

Volcano visitors

In some places, you can safely explore real volcanoes up close! In Iceland, you can even go inside the empty magma chamber of an extinct volcano.

Crater ceremonies

Some volcanoes play an important role in people's lives. In Indonesia, Mount Bromo is linked to the life of the Tenggerese people. Many of them honor the gods by throwing offerings into its crater.

Green slopes
Volcanic ash in soil can help plants grow. Farmers near the Chu Dang Ya volcano in Vietnam plant crops on its slopes, all the way into the crater.

Fireweed grows well in volcanic soil.

Out of the ashes

Volcanic eruptions can bring devastation, but they can also bring life. They clear away old, dead plants, and the ash thrown out enriches the soil, helping new plants grow quickly.

Plant power
Ferns are some of the first plants to grow after an eruption. They have very tough seeds and are able to push their way up through solid lava.

GEMSTONE GIFTS

Volcanic eruptions also bring mineral-rich materials to the surface. Gemstones such as diamonds form under heat and pressure underground, while others such as opal develop in volcanic rocks.

Diamond

Opal

Digging in

After an eruption, animals return slowly. In North and Central America, pocket gophers are often the first to arrive, digging tunnels that mix the soil and spread nutrients for plants.

Molten magic

Flowing lava is like molten magic. As it cools, it can twist into tunnels and carve out caves. Wind and water can wear down volcanic ash, leaving behind extraordinary shapes!

Fairy chimneys in the Cappadocia region of Turkey (Türkiye)

Carving caves

When lava tubes cool they can form caves called grottoes. If a grotto is near the ocean, water may enter it, forming a crystal clear pool.

Lava lair

A lava tube forms when the outer surface of a lava flow cools and hardens, leaving a tunnel for molten rock to pass through. The Búri lava tube in Iceland is famous for the ice sculptures at its entrance.

Charming chimneys

Millions of years ago, volcanoes in Turkey (Türkiye) erupted, leaving behind layers of ash and volcanic rock. Over time, the wind and rain shaped them into chimneylike towers.

The lava cooled into rocks with a six-sided, or hexagonal, shape.

Where giants walk

The Giant's Causeway in Northern Ireland formed 60 million years ago from cooling lava flows. The locals once believed that these rocks were made by a giant named Fionn MacCumhaill.

Power plume

The Hunga Tonga-Hunga-Ha'apai volcano on a Pacific Island erupted in 2022. It sent a plume of gas and ash five times higher than where passenger planes fly!

Record breakers

Many volcanoes are extraordinary, but there are some famous ones that are the biggest or most destructive ever seen on Earth. Get ready to meet the all-time greats!

Endless eruption

The volcano called Kīlauea on the island of Hawaii erupts almost all the time. Out come fountains, falls, rivers, and even a lake of lava.

More than 540 million tons (490 metric tons) of ash were thrown out during the eruption.

Lava falls off Kīlauea's rocky seaside edge.

Deadly destroyer

The 1980 eruption of Mount St. Helens in the United States was followed by the largest landslide in human history. It destroyed forests, roads, bridges, and homes.

Lake inside the crater of Mount Tambora in Indonesia

Global game-changer

In 1815, Mount Tambora blew its top with a giant boom! The ash released blocked so much sunlight that the world got colder, crops failed, and many people went hungry.

Suited and booted

To pick up burning rock samples and walk across red-hot lava, volcanologists need to wear special suits, masks, and heatproof boots.

Fiery fieldwork

A scientist who studies volcanoes is called a volcanologist. For these scientists, research can get pretty hot. In order to study a volcano, they might need to get as close as possible to its fiery heart.

Aerial assistance

Volcanologists can study eruptions from a safe distance using a flying machine called a drone. It can fly over volcanoes, take photos, and measure gases.

Tools of the trade

Scientists study and even forecast volcanic eruptions using a number of different tools. Thermal cameras spot heat, seismometers detect quakes, tiltmeters track movement of the ground, and hammers are used to collect rocks.

Seismometer

Hammer

Tiltmeter

Thermal camera

Volcanic science

Volcanoes are great for collecting samples of rock, ash, and lava. Using them, volcanologists learn how volcanoes work and how to forecast eruptions.

SOLAR SYSTEM

Earth is one of eight planets that circle our star, the sun, in a region called the solar system. Many of these planets have rocky or icy objects called moons that circle them.

Volcanic neighbors

On Earth, heat and pressure deep within the planet melts rock in the mantle to make magma, which spills out of the surface as lava in volcanic eruptions. But Earth is not the only world in space with volcanoes and underground heat!

Olympus Mons is a shield volcano.

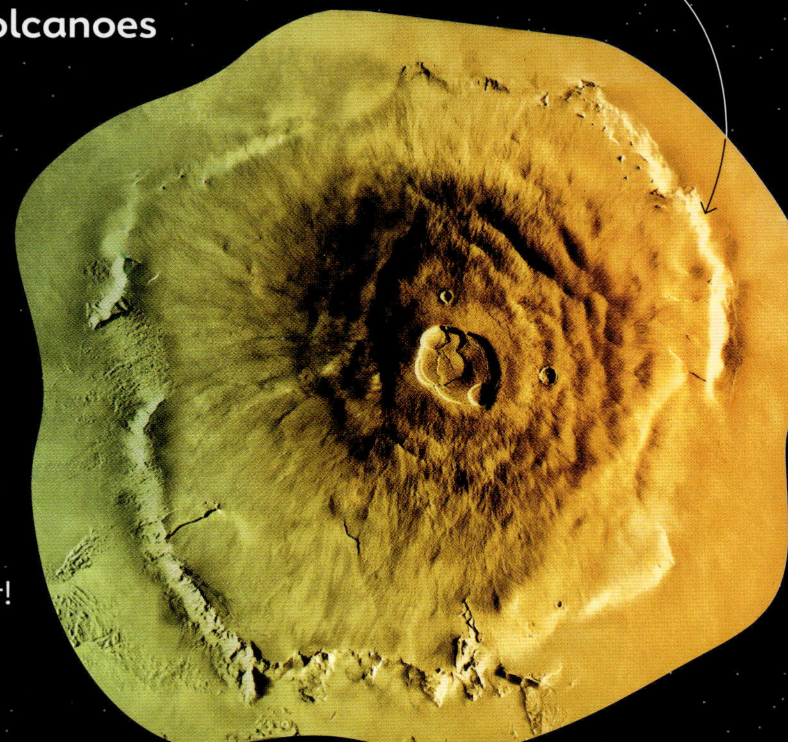

Mons-ter on Mars

The largest volcano in the solar system is Olympus Mons on Mars. It is around 400 miles (600 km) wide, and is more than twice the height of Earth's highest mountain, Mount Everest! It was active in the distant past, but is now extinct.

Incredible Io

Nowhere in the solar system has more volcanoes than Io, a moon of the giant planet Jupiter. There are hundreds on its smoldering surface, created by Jupiter's gravity squeezing and stretching its rocky mantle.

Water vapor plumes erupting on Enceladus

Ice volcanoes

Freezing-cold Enceladus—a moon of the ringed planet Saturn—has unusual volcanoes. They don't spurt out molten rock lava, but explode with a mixture of water and other chemicals instead.

Facts match

How much do you know about volcanoes? Read the clues and see if you can find the correct answers among the pictures.

1
This red-hot **liquid flows out of volcanoes** during eruptions.

7
The erosion of volcanic ash and rock made these **cone-shaped rock formations.**

8
These deep-sea creatures **thrive near underwater hydrothermal vents,** surviving without sunlight.

9
Scientists use this special **floating tool** to watch the waves.

2

Hundreds of active volcanoes **pepper the surface of this moon** of the planet Jupiter.

3

Scientists use this tool to **detect tremors**.

5

These are some of the **first plants** to grow after an eruption.

4

This rock is formed during violent eruptions. It is **light and has lots of tiny holes**.

6

Deep underground, this precious stone forms under **extremely high heat and pressure**.

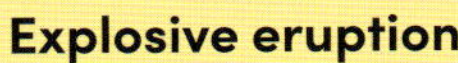

Explosive eruption

Pumice

Chimney houses

Io

Seismometer

Diamond

10

An eruption of this type **blasts ash, gas, and rock violently** into the air, often with a loud boom.

11

When Pompeii was dug up in the 1700s, this food item was found preserved in ash.

Answers: 1.Lava 2.Io 3.Seismometer 4.Pumice 5.Ferns 6.Diamond 7.Chimney houses 8.Giant tubeworms 9.Warning buoy 10.Explosive eruption 11.Preserved eggs

What's this?

Test your knowledge of volcanoes by identifying these close-up pictures. The clues will help.

3

✷ Supervolcanic eruptions formed this region 66 million years ago.

✷ It is a place in western India.

1

✷ This is the tallest mountain in Japan.

✷ It's a dormant volcano.

4

✷ A rainbow of colors is seen around this hot spring in the United States.

✷ The color comes from heat-loving life forms.

2

✷ These rock formations are found in Northern Ireland.

✷ They were created by lava flows.

5

✷ This reptile is found only on the Galápagos Islands.

✷ Its color helps it blend in with volcanic rock.

8

✷ In 1980, this volcano in the United States erupted in a huge explosion.

✷ Its eruption was followed by a large landslide.

6

✷ Lava bits in ash clouds rub together, sparking this weather event.

✷ It flashes across the sky sometimes during an eruption.

9

✷ Iceland is home to this shield volcano.

✷ It was dormant for almost 6,000 years before erupting.

7

✷ Blue flames rise from this Indonesian volcano.

✷ It has a sulfur mine.

Answers: 1.Mount Fuji 2.The Giant's Causeway 3.Deccan Traps 4.Grand Prismatic Spring 5.Lava lizard 6.Volcanic lightning 7.Mount Ijen 8.Mount St Helens 9. Fagradalsfjall

Fire trek

Find your way through a volcano park! Follow the clues to reach the big volcano at the finish line. But watch out for boulders and tricky wrong turns.

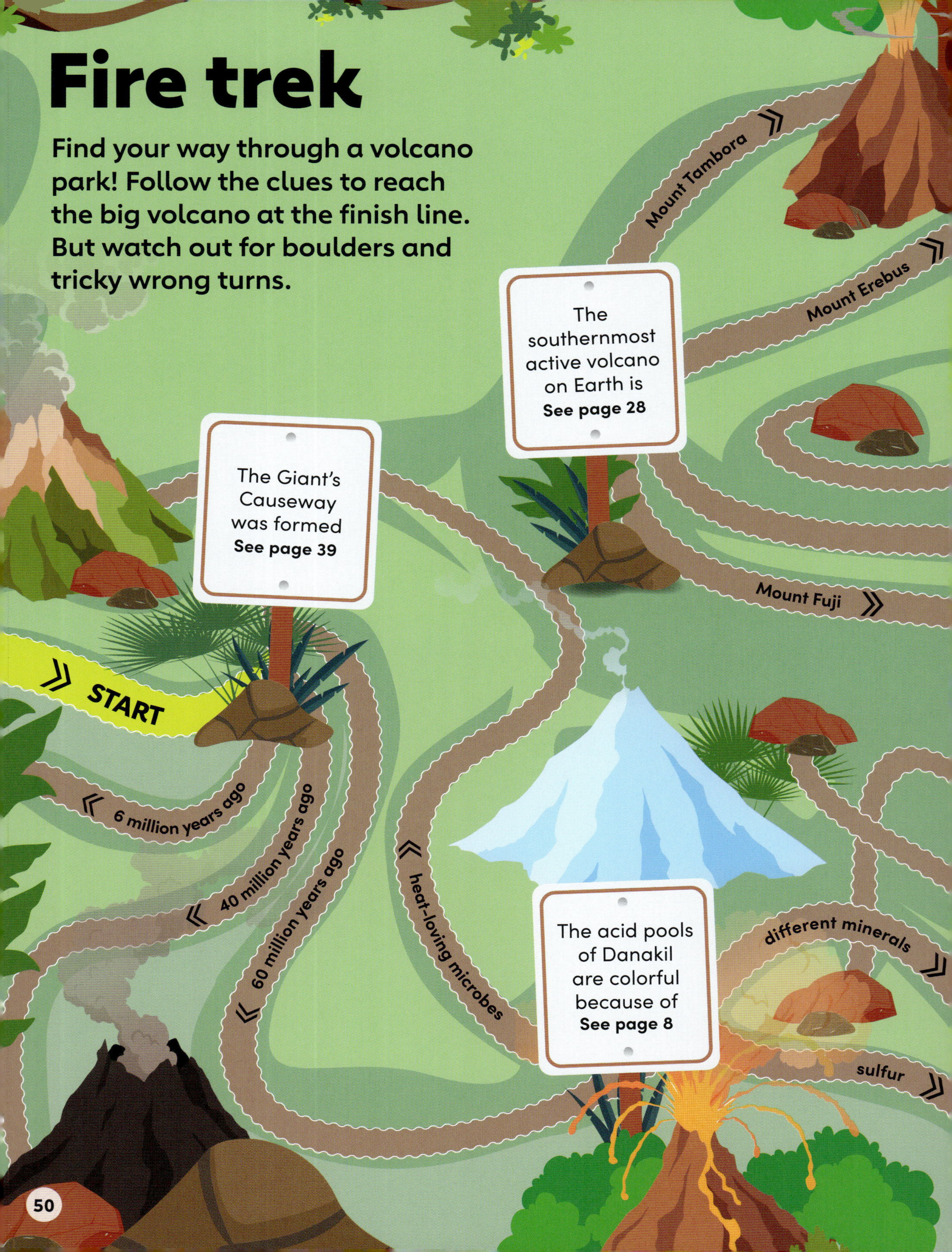

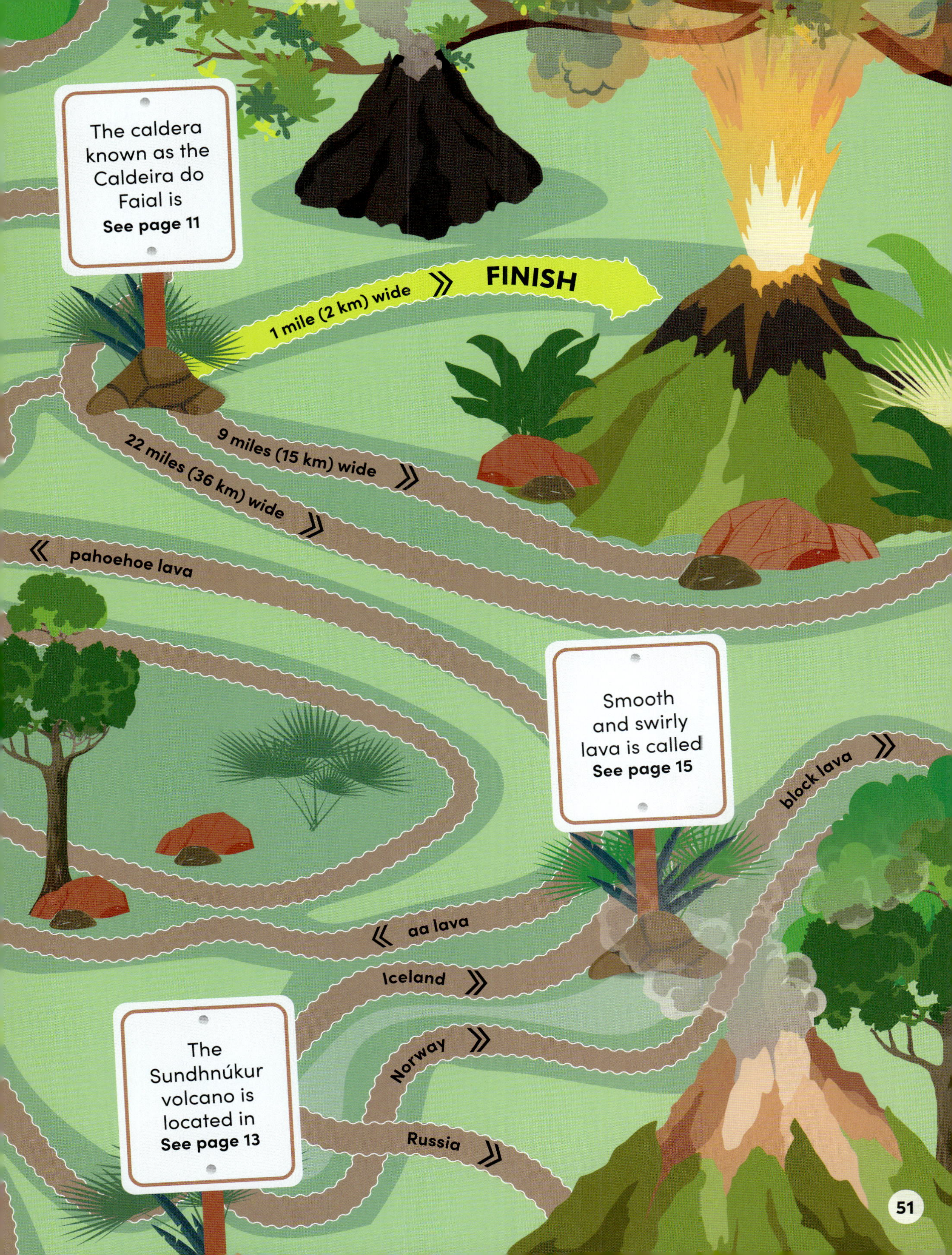

The caldera known as the Caldeira do Faial is
See page 11
1 mile (2 km) wide
FINISH
9 miles (15 km) wide
22 miles (36 km) wide
pahoehoe lava
Smooth and swirly lava is called
See page 15
block lava
aa lava
Iceland
Norway
Russia
The Sundhnúkur volcano is located in
See page 13

To the top!

Be the first to climb to the top of a volcano and look inside the fiery crater! Sidestep the steaming vents and watch out for chunks of hot volcanic ash on your way.

Finish
How to play
This is a game for up to four players.
You will need dice and counters for each player. You could use counters from other board games you might have, or you could make your own counters with colored paper—one color for each player.
Move down!
Move up!
Each player takes turns to throw the dice, and begins from the START box. Follow the squares with each roll of the dice. If you land on an instruction, make sure you do as it says. Good luck!
Steam vents point the way up. Two spaces ahead!
A lava lizard startles you. Jump back three spaces.
Watch out for the monkeys near the hot pool. Go back two spaces.
You spot a piece of shiny obsidian. Move three spaces.

Glossary

Acid A liquid with a pH less than seven. Acid can be strong enough to dissolve objects, or mild enough to eat, like lemon juice.

Archaeologist A scientist who studies history by examining objects from long ago.

Ash (volcanic) A mixture of fine volcanic material thrown out during volcanic eruptions.

Atmosphere The mixture of gases that surrounds Earth, including the air we breathe.

Buoy A floating device on the water. Some buoys can help detect and warn of tsunamis.

Caldera A large hole created when a volcano collapses after a huge eruption.

Cinder A small, rough piece of scorching hot rock thrown out of a volcano.

Crater A bowl-shaped hole at the mouth of some volcanoes.

Crust The outer, solid layer of Earth.

Dormant A volcano that isn't erupting now but might in the future.

Earthquake The violent shaking of part of Earth's surface because of tectonic plates grinding against each other. *See also* tectonic plates

Eruption When lava, ash, and gases burst or flow out of a volcano.

Extinct A volcano that will never erupt again.

Fissure A long crack or split in the ground.

Gemstone A colorful rock or mineral that can be cut and polished.

Geyser A type of hot spring that shoots a jet of water and steam into the air like a fountain.

Hot spring A natural pool of water warmed by heat from deep within Earth.

Hydrothermal vent An opening in the ocean floor where hot, mineral-rich water spurts out.

Igneous rock Rock that forms when lava cools and hardens.

Landform A natural shape on Earth's surface, such as a cave, valley, or volcano.

Landslide When a large amount of rocks, dirt, or mud suddenly slide downhill.

Lava flow A stream of lava that moves across the ground during or after an eruption.

Magma Hot molten rock beneath Earth's surface.

Magma chamber A large underground pool of molten rock that collects beneath a volcano.

Mantle The thick layer of hot rock below Earth's crust.

Mineral A naturally occurring solid found in the ground, such as gold.

Nutrient A substance that all living things need to grow.

Plume A spout of liquid or gas ejected upward in a column.

Rift A deep crack or gap in Earth's crust.

Smoldering Burning slowly with smoke but no flames.

Tectonic plates Huge pieces of Earth's crust that grind against one another as they move.

Tremor Gentle shaking from a small earthquake.

Tsunami A giant ocean wave caused by a volcanic eruption or an earthquake under the sea.

Volcanic island An island formed by lava from an underwater volcano solidifying over time and emerging out of the water.

Volcanologist A scientist who studies volcanoes and how they work.

Index

Acknowledgments

DK would like to thank the following people for their help with making the book: Jonathan Melmoth for text contributions; Shahid Qureshi for editorial assistance; Samrajkumar S for picture credits; Rakesh Kumar for DTP assistance; Sarosh Arif and DK's Inclusion & Impact Team for a sensitivity check; Laura Gilbert for proofreading; and Hilary Bird for indexing.

The publisher would like to thank the following for their kind permission to reproduce their photographs:
(Key: a-above; b-below/bottom; c-center; f-far; l-left; r-right; t-top)

1 Alamy Stock Photo: Tom Till. **2 Getty Images / iStock:** Евгений Харитонов (br). **3 Getty Images / iStock:** Pham Hung (b); theartist312 (tr). **4 Alamy Stock Photo:** Hum Images (tl). **4-5 Science Photo Library:** Claus Lunau (bc). **5 Dorling Kindersley:** NASA / Arran Lewis (tr). **6 Getty Images:** Emad Aljumah (bc). **Science Photo Library:** Claus Lunau (bl); QA International (c). **6-7 Alamy Stock Photo:** Michael Pitts / Nature Picture Library. **8 Alamy Stock Photo:** Mark Kanning (cla); Wolfgang Plankensteiner (b). **8-9 Dreamstime.com:** Alexkane1977vi (t). **9 Alamy Stock Photo:** Jason Lindsey (cr); Tom Till (bc). **10-11 Alamy Stock Photo:** Creston Medprous (ca); Dominic Byrne (b). **Dreamstime.com:** Javarman (c). **Getty Images:** AFP / Mario Vazquez (tc). **12 Getty Images:** Sheldovitsky Artem Igorevich / IViS / Handout / Anadolu (bl). **12-13 Alamy Stock Photo:** Almannavarnadeild / Icelandic Civil Defense. **13 Alamy Stock Photo:** Wyatt Mayo / Associated Press (br). **Getty Images / iStock:** Eloi_Omella (t). **14-15 naturepl.com:** Will Burrard-Lucas (b). **15 Alamy Stock Photo:** Brad Lewis / RGB Ventures / SuperStock (tr); Doug Perrine (crb); Maximilian Buzun (cr); Kevin Schafer / Minden Pictures (cra). **Dreamstime.com:** Rob Kemp (tc). **16 Alamy Stock Photo:** Colin Munro (br). **Dreamstime.com:** Elena Leusik (cl). **17 Getty Images / iStock:** gadaian (t). **18-19 Alamy Stock Photo:** Michael Brooks. **18 Bridgeman Images:** The Holbarn Archive (tr). **Dorling Kindersley:** Museo Archeologico Nazionale di Napoli / James Stevenson (cla). **19 Alamy Stock Photo:** funkyfood London - Paul Williams (cr). **Dreamstime.com:** Richard Villalon (tr). **20-21 Alamy Stock Photo:** Francisco Negroni (t). **20 Alamy Stock Photo:** Barry Lewis (br). **21 Alamy Stock Photo:** Francisco Negroni (tr). **Getty Images:** Sygma / Langevin Jacques (br). **22 Getty Images:** AFP / Nurul Hidayat (cl). **Shutterstock.com:** Tsyntseus Anastasiia (tr). **22-23 Getty Images:** Kyodo News (b). **23 Dreamstime.com:** Linda Lim (tc). **24 Alamy Stock Photo:** Imagebroker.com / S Jonasson (tl). **24-25 Getty Images:** Alexis Rosenfeld (bc). **25 Alamy Stock Photo:** Jason O. Watson (t). **Dreamstime.com:** Jesse Kraft (c). **26 Alamy Stock Photo:** ZUMA Press, Inc. / Arnold Drapkin (t). **Dreamstime.com:** Bernadett Pogácsás-Simon (cra). **Getty Images:** LightRocket / Fred Ihrt (crb). **27 Alamy Stock Photo:** Ingo Oeland (b). **Getty Images:** NordicPhotos (cla). **28 Alamy Stock Photo:** Art Directors / Andrew Gasson (t). **28-29 Getty Images / iStock:** Mazzzur (b). **29 Dreamstime.com:** Sihasakprachum (crb). **NASA:** Jeff Schmaltz, LANCE / EOSDIS MODIS Rapid Response Team / GSFC (tr). **30-31 Alamy Stock Photo:** Nature Picture Library / Yukihiro Fukuda (t). **30 Alamy Stock Photo:** Galih (crb). **31 Alamy Stock Photo:** Rosanne Tackaberry (b). **naturepl.com:** Nature Production (tr). **32 Courtesy of Smithsonian. ©2023 Smithsonian:** Lee Siebert, 1994 (Smithsonian Institution) (bl). **Science Photo Library:** Claus Lunau (tl). **32-33 Science Photo Library:** CNES, 2001 Distribution Spot Image (t). **33 Alamy Stock Photo:** Dinodia Photos (b). **U.S. Geological Survey:** Dougal Townsend (cr). **34 Alamy Stock Photo:** Hemis / Bourseiller Philippe (tr). **34-35 Getty Images:** AFP / Juni Kriswanto. **35 Alamy Stock Photo:** Poelzer Wolfgang (tr). **Olga Shevchenko:** (cla). **36 Dreamstime.com:** Amy Nicolai (crb). **Getty Images / iStock:** Digitalvision Vectors / Ivan-96 (cl). **36-37 Getty Images / iStock:** Pham Hung (t). **37 Dreamstime.com:** Roberto Junior (clb); Vvoevale (cb). **Getty Images / iStock:** Oleg Spiridonov (br). **38-39 Alamy Stock Photo:** Funkyfood London - Paul Williams (t). **38 Dreamstime.com:** SimonDannhauer (bl). **39 Alamy Stock Photo:** Cavan Images (tr). **Getty Images:** Stone / Andrea Pistolesi (br). **40 Getty Images:** Maxar (tl); Photodisc / Stocktrek (cr). **40-41 Dreamstime.com:** Muda Com (b). **41 Getty Images / iStock:** theartist312 (tr). **42 Alamy Stock Photo:** Media Drum World. **43 Alamy Stock Photo:** SciTech Image / James King-Holmes (c); VWPics / Nano Calvo (c/Tiltmeter). **Dreamstime.com:** Alexander Piragis (tr). **Getty Images / iStock:** Bestgreenscreen (c/ Thermal Camera); Евгений Харитонов (br). **Shutterstock.com:** Ari_Susanti (c/ Hammer). **44 Alamy Stock Photo:** Science History Images / Photo Researchers (br). **44-45 Getty Images:** Future / All About Space; Stocktrek Images / Ron Miller (t). **45 Getty Images / iStock:** Elen11 (cl). **46 Alamy Stock Photo:** Galih (cra); Ingo Oeland (c). **Depositphotos Inc:** Dewins (ca). **Dorling Kindersley:** Museo Archeologico Nazionale di Napoli / James Stevenson (cb). **Dreamstime.com:** Linda Lim (cl). **47 Alamy Stock Photo:** SciTech Image / James King-Holmes (cr). **Dreamstime.com:** Elen33 (ca); Rob Kemp (clb); Roberto Junior (cb). **Getty Images / iStock:** Smitt (c). **48 Alamy Stock Photo:** Adam Burton (clb); Dinodia Photos (tr); Stefano Politi Markovina (cla); Peter Adams Photography (crb). **49 Adobe Stock:** 24K-Production (cr); Emmajay1 (tl). **Alamy Stock Photo:** Ann Ronan Picture Library / Photo12 (tr); Hemis / Godin Stéphane (clb). **Getty Images:** Moment / Mariano Sayno (cl). **50-51 Adobe Stock:** The8monkey. **52 Dreamstime.com:** Alexander Piragis (ca). **Getty Images / iStock:** Digitalvision Vectors / Ivan-96 (crb); Hector Milla (cl). **52-53 Dreamstime.com:** Rudzhan Nagiev (Background). **53 Adobe Stock:** Teayataka (crb). **Dreamstime.com:** Steve Allen (cla); Sergey Uryadnikov (cl); Mahira (bc). **54-55 Getty Images / iStock:** Eloi_Omella

Cover images: *Front:* **123RF.com:** Alexmax bl; **Alamy Stock Photo:** Derek Anderson cra, Blue Planet Archive BPA cr/ (Polychaete), Blue Planet Archive LLC crb/ (Tube Worm), Hemis / Spani Arnaud tc/ (Flower), Alex Ramsay ca, Tom Till cr; **Dreamstime.com:** Elen33 crb, Sergey Galushko tr, Vvoevale cl/ (Dacite Rock); **Getty Images:** Tetra images / Jed Share / Kaoru Share br; **Getty Images / iStock:** DancingMan c; **Science Photo Library:** NASA / Carnegie Mellon University cl; **Shutterstock.com:** Sebastian Janicki cra/ (Agate), clb/ (Sulphur Stone), Dario Lo Presti tc, Michail_Vorobyev clb; **SuperStock:** Image Asset Management / World History Archive tl; *Back:* **Alamy Stock Photo:** Galih cra; **Dorling Kindersley:** NASA / Arran Lewis tl; **Dreamstime.com:** Michal Baranski bc, Roberto Junior cla, Richard Villalon tc, Vvoevale crb; **Getty Images:** Corbis Documentary / Atlantide Phototravel bl; **Getty Images / iStock:** Bestgreenscreen cr, Digitalvision Vectors / Ivan-96 cl, Smitt tc/ (Cappadocia); **naturepl.com:** Joel Sartore 2025 tr; **Shutterstock.com:** Ari_Susanti bc/ (Hammer), Zaven Sargsyan br; **U.S. Geological Survey:** Christoph Kern clb; *Spine:* **Getty Images / iStock:** DancingMan